WEEKLY WR READER®
EARLY LEARNING LIBRARY

LIFE LONG AGO

The Middle Ages

by Tea Benduhn

Reading consultant: Susan Nations, M.Ed.,
author/literacy coach/consultant in literacy development

Please visit our web site at: www.garethstevens.com
For a free color catalog describing Weekly Reader® Early Learning Library's list
of high-quality books, call 1-877-445-5824 (USA) or 1-800-387-3178 (Canada).
Weekly Reader® Early Learning Library's fax: (414) 336-0164.

Library of Congress Cataloging-in-Publication Data

Benduhn, Tea.
    The Middle Ages / by Tea Benduhn.
        p. cm. — (Life long ago)
    Includes bibliographical references and index.
    ISBN-13: 978-0-8368-7784-7 (lib. bdg.)
    ISBN-13: 978-0-8368-7789-2 (softcover)
    1. Middle Ages—Juvenile literature. 2. Civilization, Medieval—Juvenile literature. I. Title.
    CB351.B46   2006
    909.07—dc22   2006030348

This edition first published in 2007 by
Weekly Reader® Early Learning Library
A Member of the WRC Media Family of Companies
330 West Olive Street, Suite 100
Milwaukee, WI 53212 USA

Copyright © 2007 by Weekly Reader® Early Learning Library

Managing editor: Valerie J. Weber
Art direction: Tammy West
Cover design, page layout, and illustrations: Dave Kowalski
Picture research: Diane Laska-Swanke

Picture credits: Cover, title, © John Stevens/Ancient Art & Architecture Collection; pp. 4, 6, 8, 18 © North Wind Picture Archives; pp. 5, 15 © Prisma/Ancient Art & Architecture Collection; p. 7 Dave Kowalski/© Weekly Reader Early Learning Library; p. 9 © Historical Picture Archive/CORBIS; pp. 10, 21 © Brian Gibbs/Ancient Art & Architecture Collection; pp. 11, 13 © Ronald Sheridan/Ancient Art & Architecture Collection; pp. 12, 14, 16 © The Granger Collection, New York; p. 17 © Brian Wilson/Ancient Art & Architecture Collection; p. 19 © Index/Ancient Art & Architecture Collection; p. 20 © Ancient Art & Architecture Collection

Printed in the United States of America

1 2 3 4 5 6 7 8 9 10 10 09 08 07 06

TABLE OF CONTENTS

Cover and Title Page: Bodiam Castle was built in Sussex, England, in 1385, near the end of the Middle Ages. A moat surrounds the castle.

CHAPTER 1

What Are the Middle Ages?

Have you ever seen a knight in shining armor? Knights rode horses into battle. They worked for a king who lived in a castle. You may have seen knights, kings, and castles in a movie about the Middle Ages. Movies make the Middle Ages seem like a time filled with adventure.

© North Wind Picture Archives

Many people lived and worked in a castle. The royal family had lots of servants who took care of the horses, cooking, cleaning, and other duties.

Most people living in the Middle Ages, however, did not think their lives were filled with adventure. They stayed near their birthplace their entire lives. Many people were farmers, but few owned their own farms. Most farmed land that belonged to wealthy people.

Peasants farmed with simple tools during the Middle Ages. Here, one man cuts hay with a scythe, a sharp, curved blade at the end of a pole.

King Henry II dressed like many other kings during the Middle Ages. He wore a crown and fancy robes made with gold thread and decorated with jewels.

The Middle Ages lasted from about A.D. 500 to 1500. During that time, many different kings ruled large areas of land. The area that these kings ruled is known as **medieval** Europe.

The people living in medieval Europe had similar ideas and ways of life. Today, the lands of medieval Europe are known as modern Europe, northern Africa, and the western parts of Asia.

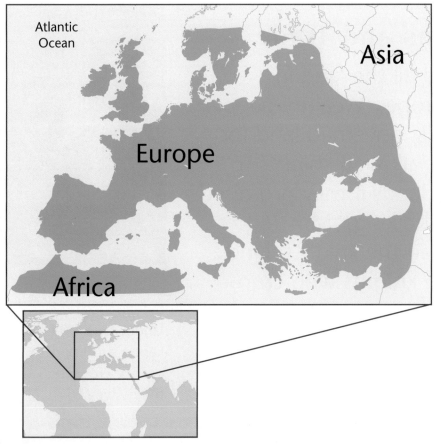

Atlantic Ocean

Asia

Europe

Africa

The dark green area of the map shows where people lived in medieval Europe.

CHAPTER 2

Towns and Trade

Kings owned all the land in medieval Europe. Wealthy people, such as **lords**, governed land for kings. Lords allowed knights to live on their lands if they promised to fight for the king. Most other people farmed the knights' land and paid the knights with crops. In return, the knights protected them from attack. This system is called **feudalism**.

© North Wind Picture Archives

Peasants farmed the land for the landowners. They kept a small part of their crops for themselves.

In the beginning of the Middle Ages, most people lived in the country. Some traveled from town to town to trade food, clothes, and tools. People known as merchants used money to trade for items. They met in towns known as trading centers. The towns grew into large cities.

People sold items such as shoes, cloth, and dishes in a covered market in fifteenth-century Europe.

Some towns had walls built around them for protection from attack. A church stood in the middle of the town. Christianity was the main religion in medieval Europe during the Middle Ages. The Christian Church came up with the rules for people to live by. Even kings had to follow these rules.

A large church, Ely Cathedral was built in Cambridgeshire, England, during the Middle Ages.

Some people followed different religions. Many Jews lived in Europe during the Middle Ages. Islam was born during the Middle Ages. Muslims moved from North Africa and into southern Spain in A.D. 800. Muslim lands stretched into the Middle East and Central Asia.

A stained-glass window shows medieval European Jews as scientists, bankers, translators, engineers, pharmacists, and brewers.

CHAPTER 3

Family Life

If you lived during the Middle Ages, you would probably work a full-time job by the time you turned twelve years old. At fifteen, you would probably get married. By twenty, you might have children of your own. Many people did not live past the age of thirty or thirty-five.

Whole families, such as these cabinet makers, worked together at a craft.

Children played games such as swinging, spinning tops, and skittles, a type of bowling.

People often had lots of children, but many did not make it beyond their first birthday. Those that lived often played games such as follow-the-leader, horseshoes, and checkers. Children also started learning prayers at a very young age.

At the age of seven, children in wealthy families were allowed to go to school. Most other children began training as **apprentices**. A boy learned his father's skill as a merchant, blacksmith, carpenter, farmer, or other kind of worker. Girls learned from their mothers how to weave, do chores, or cook.

In a German school for boys, students crowded onto benches, waiting for their turn with a teacher.

People worked hard to stay alive. Farmers had to give most of their crops to wealthy land owners. Merchants paid high taxes to lords. Few people were wealthy enough to get an education. Educated people could become doctors, lawyers, and clergy.

Workers plowed fields outside a city in fifteenth-century rural Italy. Their working days were long and hard. Many died young.

Many people lived in houses made of mud or wood with a roof made of hay. Mice and other pests crawled throughout the house. The streets were littered with garbage. Food spoiled easily, and people often got sick from food poisoning. When people got sick, they usually died.

People build their houses of wood outside the castle's sturdy stone walls.

The number-one killer during the Middle Ages was the **bubonic plague**. Rats carried the plague. Fleas spread the plague from rats to humans. People usually died within hours of being bitten by the fleas.

So many people died during the bubonic plague that the living had to load carts with the dead to get them out of the streets.

CHAPTER 4

What Did We Learn from the Middle Ages?

Many modern languages started in the Middle Ages. Medieval European languages changed when people traveled. Travelers brought their languages to new lands and brought new words home. Many words in English come from German, French, Danish, and Celtic.

© North Wind Picture Archives

People traveled long distances by foot, on boats, or by riding horses or even camels. They brought back new goods and new words from their trips.

Christopher Columbus sailed his ships to new lands. He brought back riches and stories for the rulers who sent him.

We still learn from books and movies about important people from the Middle Ages. Travelers such as Christopher Columbus and Marco Polo explored the world and learned about new lands. The story of Robin Hood was even based on real people!

Do you use money or go to the bank? Before the Middle Ages, most people traded one item for another. During the Middle Ages, people began using money to trade for goods. People wanted to borrow money or keep their money in a safe place. The first banks started during the Middle Ages to keep money in.

Medieval traders exchanged their money in a money house, later known as a bank.

St. John's College was built in Cambridge, England, during the Middle Ages.

Do you want to go to college when you get older? Some of the world's most famous universities started in Paris in France and in Oxford and Cambridge in Britain during the Middle Ages. Many of the subjects taught then are still taught today. Next time you learn grammar, math, or music, you are learning from the Middle Ages!

GLOSSARY

apprentices — young people who learn a job from someone who knows the job well

birthplace — the area where someone is born

bubonic plague — a disease that spread quickly through medieval Europe and killed huge numbers of people

Celtic — a language spoken by people in what is now Great Britain during the Middle Ages

Christianity — a religion based on belief in Jesus Christ and his teachings

clergy — officials or leaders of the Christian Church

feudalism — a political system in which farmers and other workers served a lord who protected them in return

governed — made sure people followed the rules and paid taxes

grammar — the study of spelling and writing correct sentences

Islam — a religion based on belief in Allah, or God

Jews — people who follow Judaism, a belief in one God and the teachings of the Bible's Old Testament

lords — powerful, wealthy landowners

medieval — of or relating to the Middle Ages

merchants — people who buy, sell, and trade goods

Muslims — people who follow the teachings of Islam

FOR MORE INFORMATION

Books

Discovering Castle Days. The Discovery Series (series).
 J. Bradley Cruxton and W. Doug Wilson (Skyline Books)

Kids in the Middle Ages. Kids Throughout History (series).
 Lisa A. Wroble (PowerKids Press)

Knights. All Aboard Reading (series). Catherine Daly-Weir
 (Grosset & Dunlap)

Knights and Castles. Magic Tree House Research Guides
 (series). Will Osborne (Random House Books for
 Young Readers)

Web Site

Kids' Castle
www.kidsonthenet.org.uk/castle/view.html
Click anywhere on the castle to find out more about the
different people who lived during the Middle Ages.

Publisher's note to educators and parents: Our editors have carefully reviewed this
Web site to ensure that it is suitable for children. Many Web sites change frequently, however,
and we cannot guarantee that a site's future contents will continue to meet our high standards
of quality and educational value. Be advised that children should be closely supervised
whenever they access the Internet.

INDEX

About the Author

Tea Benduhn writes and edits books for children and teens. Her book reviews, author interviews, and articles have appeared in magazines and newspapers. She lives in the beautiful state of Wisconsin.